MONSTER MACHINES

Caroline Bingham

DK

DORLING KINDERSLEY
London • New York • Moscow • Sydney

A Dorling Kindersley Book

Project Editor	Shaila Awan
Art Editor	Susan St. Louis
Managing Editor	Sarah Phillips
Managing Art Editor	C. David Gillingwater
Production	Josie Alabaster
Picture Research	Maureen Sheerin
Photography	Richard Leeney
Additional Photography	Geoff Brightling, Mike Dunning
Jacket Design	Richard Czapnik
Consultant	Jack Challoner

First published in Great Britain in 1998
by Dorling Kindersley Limited,
9 Henrietta Street, London WC2E 8PS

2 4 6 8 10 9 7 5 3 1

Visit us on the World Wide Web at
http://www.dk.com

Copyright © 1998 Dorling Kindersley Limited, London

All rights reserved. No part of this publication
may be reproduced, stored in a retrieval system,
or transmitted in any form or by any means,
electronic, mechanical, photocopying, recording
or otherwise, without the prior written permission
of the copyright owner.

A CIP catalogue record for this book
is available from the British Library.

ISBN: 0-7513-5692-1

Colour reproduction by Flying Colours, Italy.
Printed and bound in Italy by Mondadori.

Dorling Kindersley would like to thank:
Ainscough Crane Hire Ltd;
British Aerospace Airbus Ltd; Airbus Industrie;
City of Mount Vernon Fire Department, NY;
Daimler-Benz Aerospace Airbus GmbH; Robert Ellis;
Halls Automotive; Live Promotions Ltd; Miller Mining.

The publisher would like to thank the following for their kind
permission to reproduce their photographs:
c=centre, t=top, b=bottom, l=left, r=right

Alvey and Towers Picture Library: 18-19c;
Camera Press: 20tl; **J. Allan Cash**: 18tl;
Bruce Coleman Ltd/Dr. Eckart Pott: 14-15c;
Getty Images: 11tr, 19tr; **Nick Hall Collection**: 15tr;
Images: 28tl; **Andrew Morland**: 31tr;
NASA: 10-11c; **Novosti (London)**: 14tl;
Stock Market/John S. Adams 12 tr;
Mark Wagner: 8tl, 8-11b, 8-10tc.

Monster truck   4

Mining shovel   6

Jumbo jet   8

Mobile crane   12

Icebreaker 14

Giant dump truck 16

Locomotive 18

Fire engine 20

Cargo plane 24

Recovery truck 26

Tractor 28

Articulated truck 30

Glossary 32

Monster truck

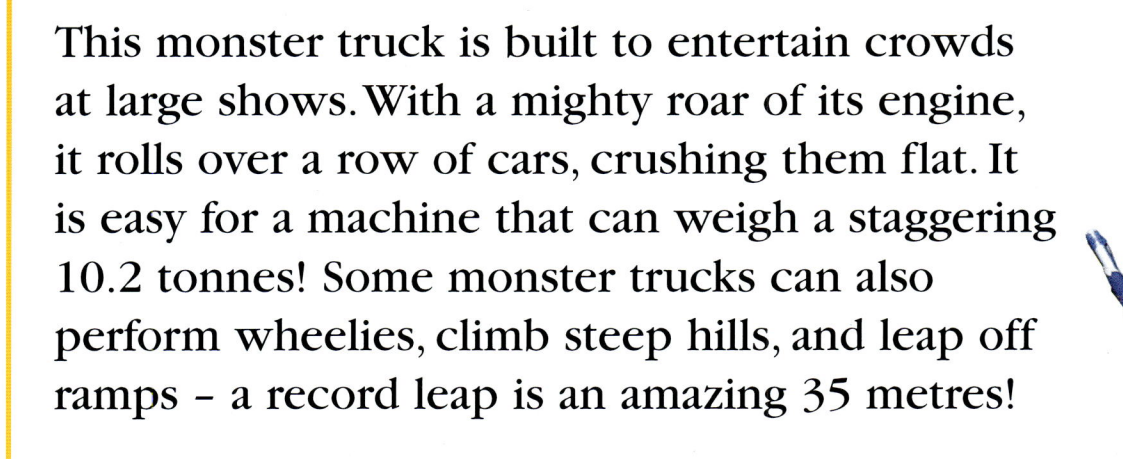

This monster truck is built to entertain crowds at large shows. With a mighty roar of its engine, it rolls over a row of cars, crushing them flat. It is easy for a machine that can weigh a staggering 10.2 tonnes! Some monster trucks can also perform wheelies, climb steep hills, and leap off ramps – a record leap is an amazing 35 metres!

A row of lights across the top of the truck is for show and for lighting the way at night events

A strong roll bar protects the driver should the truck flip over

The largest trucks stand over 4 m tall

Fibreglass body

One of a kind
No two monster trucks are the same. If you want a giant truck, you will have to design one, obtain all the parts, and then build it. Some have pick-up truck bodies, others use vans. One truck has wheels almost double the height of those shown here.

Each tyre is 1.68 m high – that's almost four times the width of a car tyre

Wheel hubs are more than 30 cm deep

Large wheels stop the truck's body from being damaged by twisted metal

The wheels make the truck over 3 m wide

Deep treads for grip in mud

A touch of glass
The truck's body is made of fibreglass, a plastic that contains fine strands of glass. This is lighter in weight than a metal body, but incredibly tough.

The body is that of a pick-up truck

This monster truck is leaping into the air in order to clear a row of cars – one of the cars has already been crushed.

This bonnet tilts forwards to allow engine access

Shock absorbers on each wheel ease movement over bumpy ground

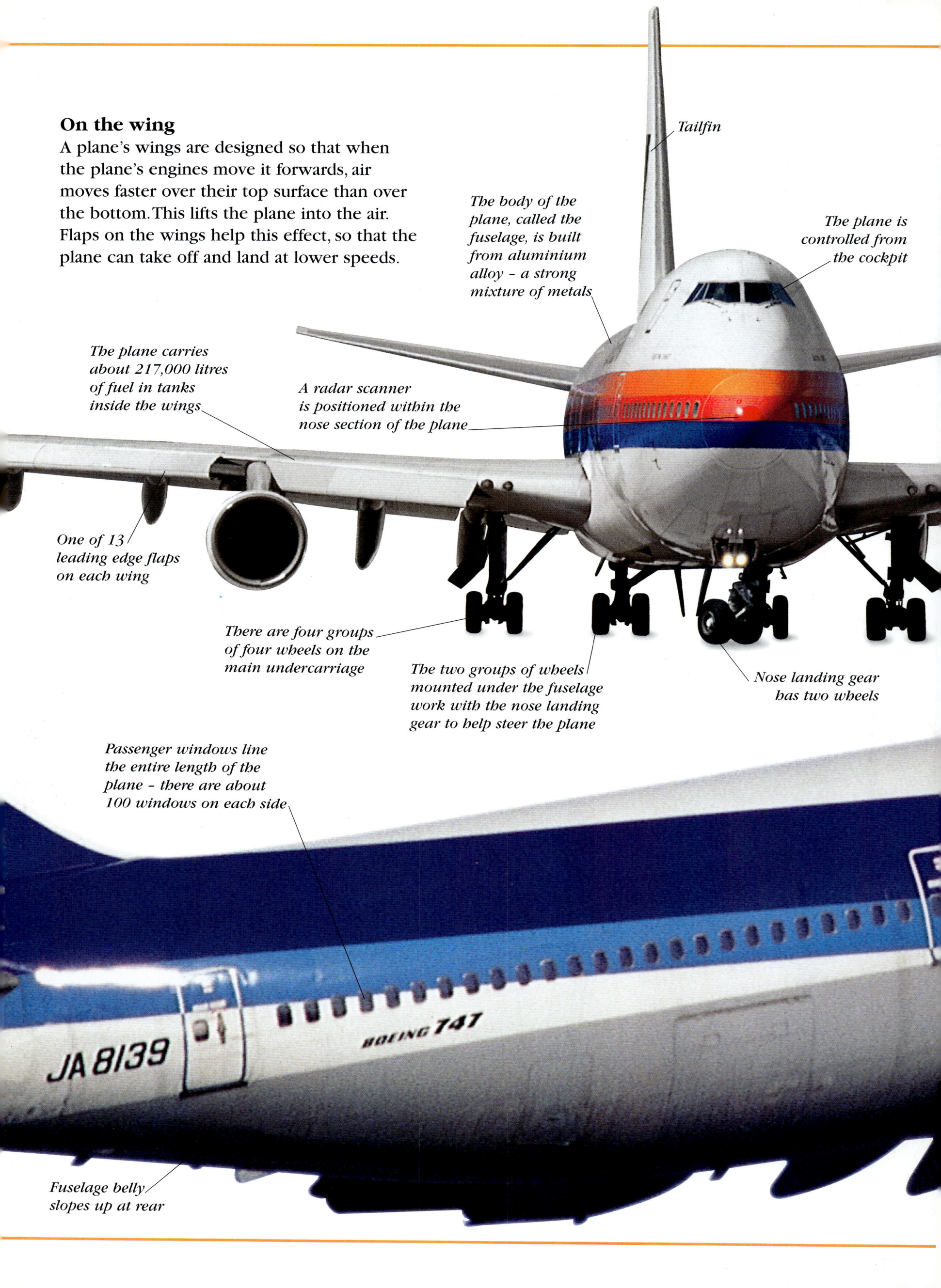

On the wing
A plane's wings are designed so that when the plane's engines move it forwards, air moves faster over their top surface than over the bottom. This lifts the plane into the air. Flaps on the wings help this effect, so that the plane can take off and land at lower speeds.

Tailfin

The body of the plane, called the fuselage, is built from aluminium alloy - a strong mixture of metals

The plane is controlled from the cockpit

The plane carries about 217,000 litres of fuel in tanks inside the wings

A radar scanner is positioned within the nose section of the plane

One of 13 leading edge flaps on each wing

There are four groups of four wheels on the main undercarriage

The two groups of wheels mounted under the fuselage work with the nose landing gear to help steer the plane

Nose landing gear has two wheels

Passenger windows line the entire length of the plane - there are about 100 windows on each side

Fuselage belly slopes up at rear

Jumbo jet

The Boeing 747 is the largest passenger plane in the world – the latest version can carry up to 570 passengers and all their luggage! The plane travels at about 978 kilometres per hour, which is very close to the speed of sound. And those enormous wings together cover an area almost the size of two tennis courts. It certainly is a jumbo jet!

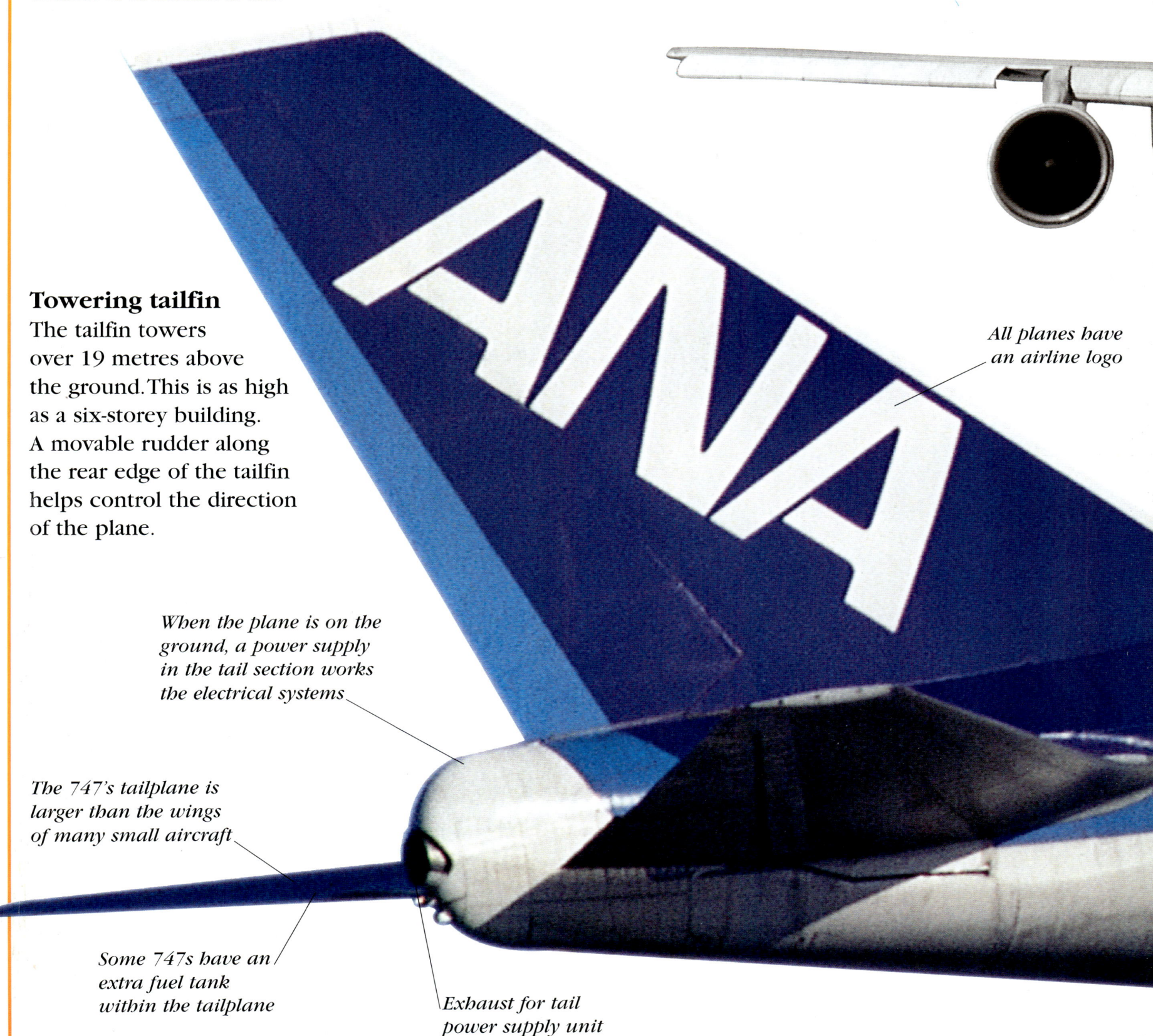

The jumbo jet is so-called because of its mammoth size.

Towering tailfin
The tailfin towers over 19 metres above the ground. This is as high as a six-storey building. A movable rudder along the rear edge of the tailfin helps control the direction of the plane.

All planes have an airline logo

When the plane is on the ground, a power supply in the tail section works the electrical systems

The 747's tailplane is larger than the wings of many small aircraft

Some 747s have an extra fuel tank within the tailplane

Exhaust for tail power supply unit

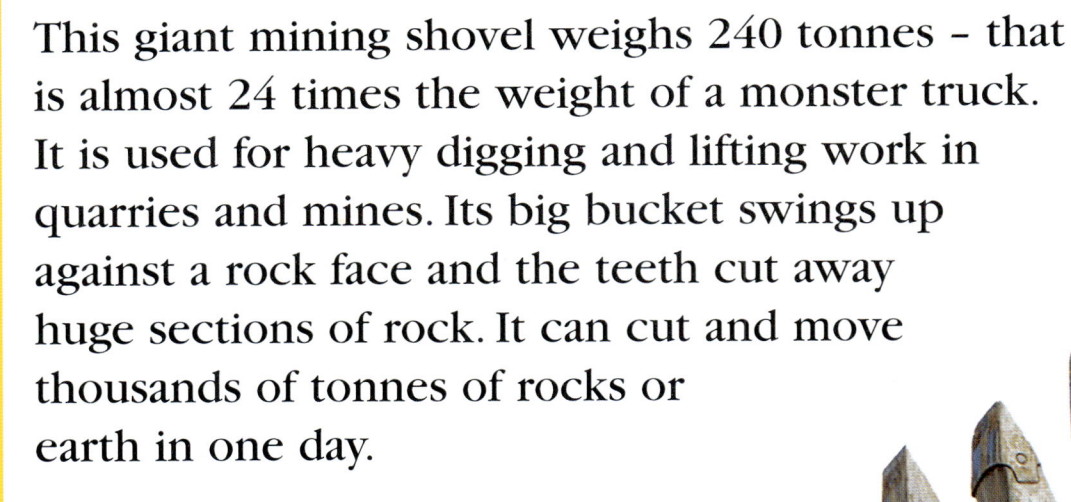

Mining shovel

This giant mining shovel weighs 240 tonnes – that is almost 24 times the weight of a monster truck. It is used for heavy digging and lifting work in quarries and mines. Its big bucket swings up against a rock face and the teeth cut away huge sections of rock. It can cut and move thousands of tonnes of rocks or earth in one day.

Dipper arm

The front half of the bucket swings open on this hinge

Sharp metal teeth can be replaced when they wear out

The bucket opens so that the load can be dropped into the back of a dump truck

Liquid strength

The boom, dipper arm, and huge bucket are moved by hydraulic rams. The rams work because liquids are squeezed along tubes inside them. This creates a pressure, or force, strong enough to make the rams move. You can clearly see the hydraulic rams working the boom and dipper arm in the picture below.

This hydraulic ram raises and lowers the dipper arm

The bucket's jaws open more than the width of a car

Brick patterning reduces wear

The cab is soundproofed and air-conditioned

A mining shovel's body can turn a full circle on top of its crawler tracks

The bottom hydraulic ram tilts the bucket

The side hydraulic ram raises and lowers the boom

Metal crawler tracks are 7.8 m long

Step ladder

Boom

A mining shovel can fill a giant dump truck with only three or four swings of its bucket.

Powerful spotlight for night work

What a load!
A mining shovel will fill a giant dump truck in a matter of minutes. That's because each bucket-load carries the equivalent in weight of almost five adult elephants!

Safety rail prevents accidents – it's about 4 m to the ground

These doors open to the engine bay

7

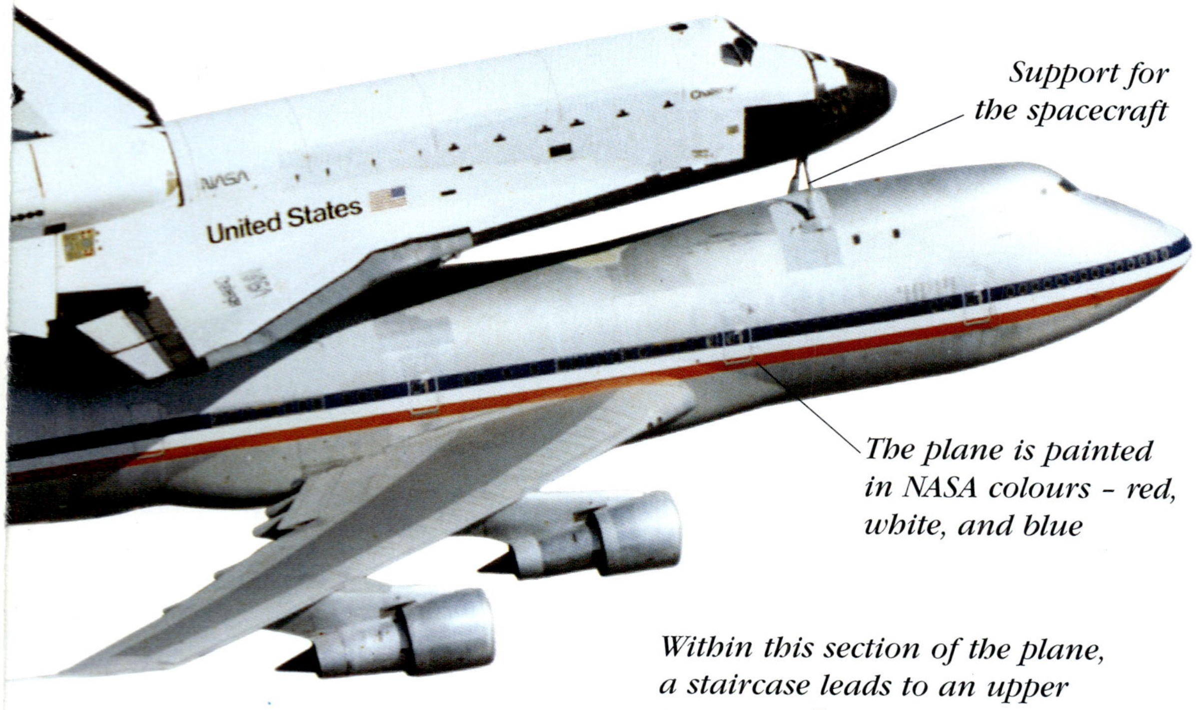

Support for the spacecraft

The plane is painted in NASA colours – red, white, and blue

The adapted 747 is known as the Shuttle Carrier Aircraft.

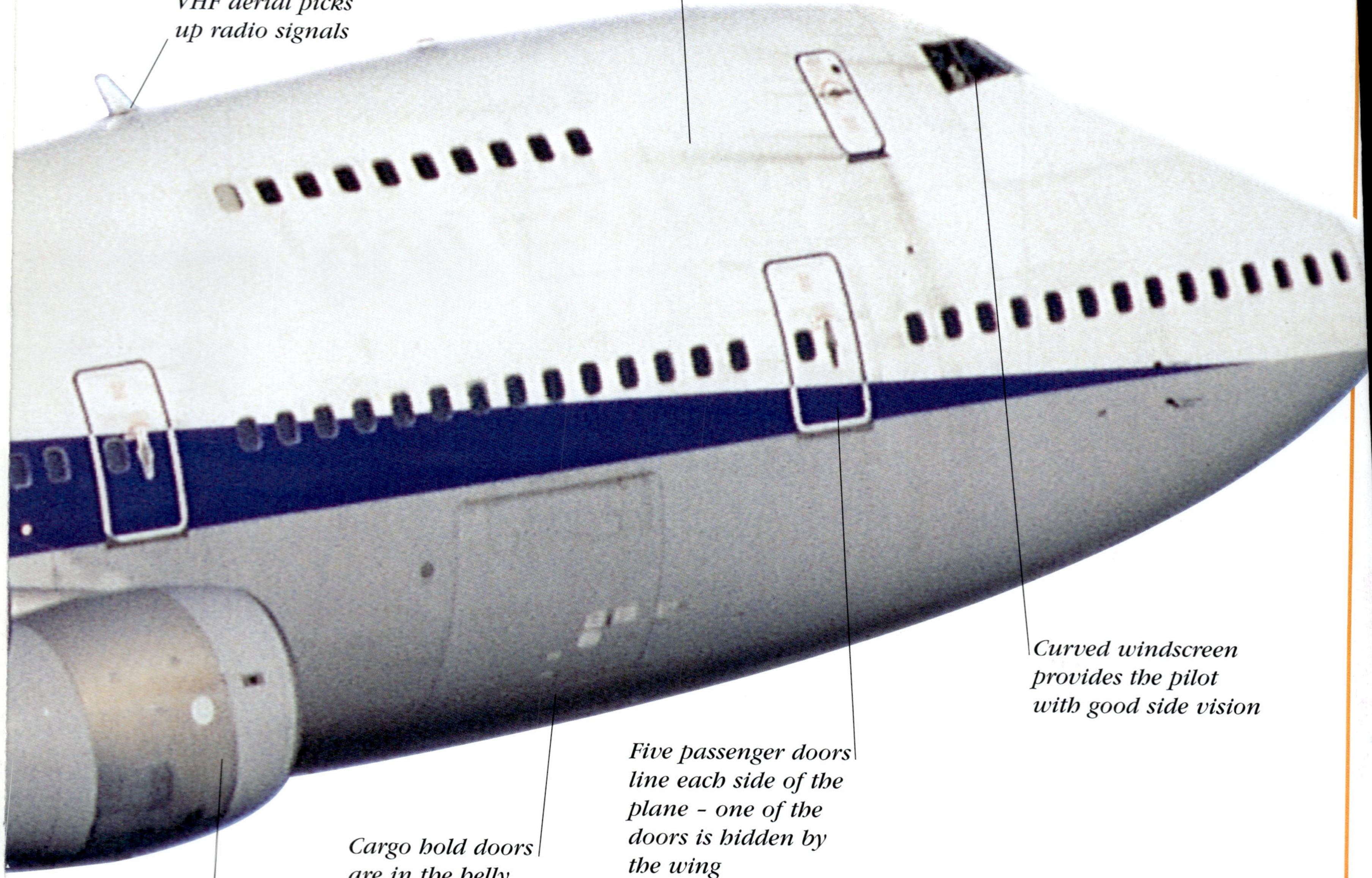

Within this section of the plane, a staircase leads to an upper passenger floor

VHF aerial picks up radio signals

Curved windscreen provides the pilot with good side vision

Five passenger doors line each side of the plane - one of the doors is hidden by the wing

Cargo hold doors are in the belly of the fuselage

One of four turbofan engines

The invisible pilot

The cockpit towers ten metres above the ground. Unlike the rest of the plane, the cockpit is very small. It seats a crew of three: two pilots and one flight engineer. A 747 is also fitted with an autopilot, which takes over on a flight to steer a course and maintain the plane's speed. In poor conditions, such as fog or thick snow, an autopilot will help take off or land the plane.

Piggyback rides

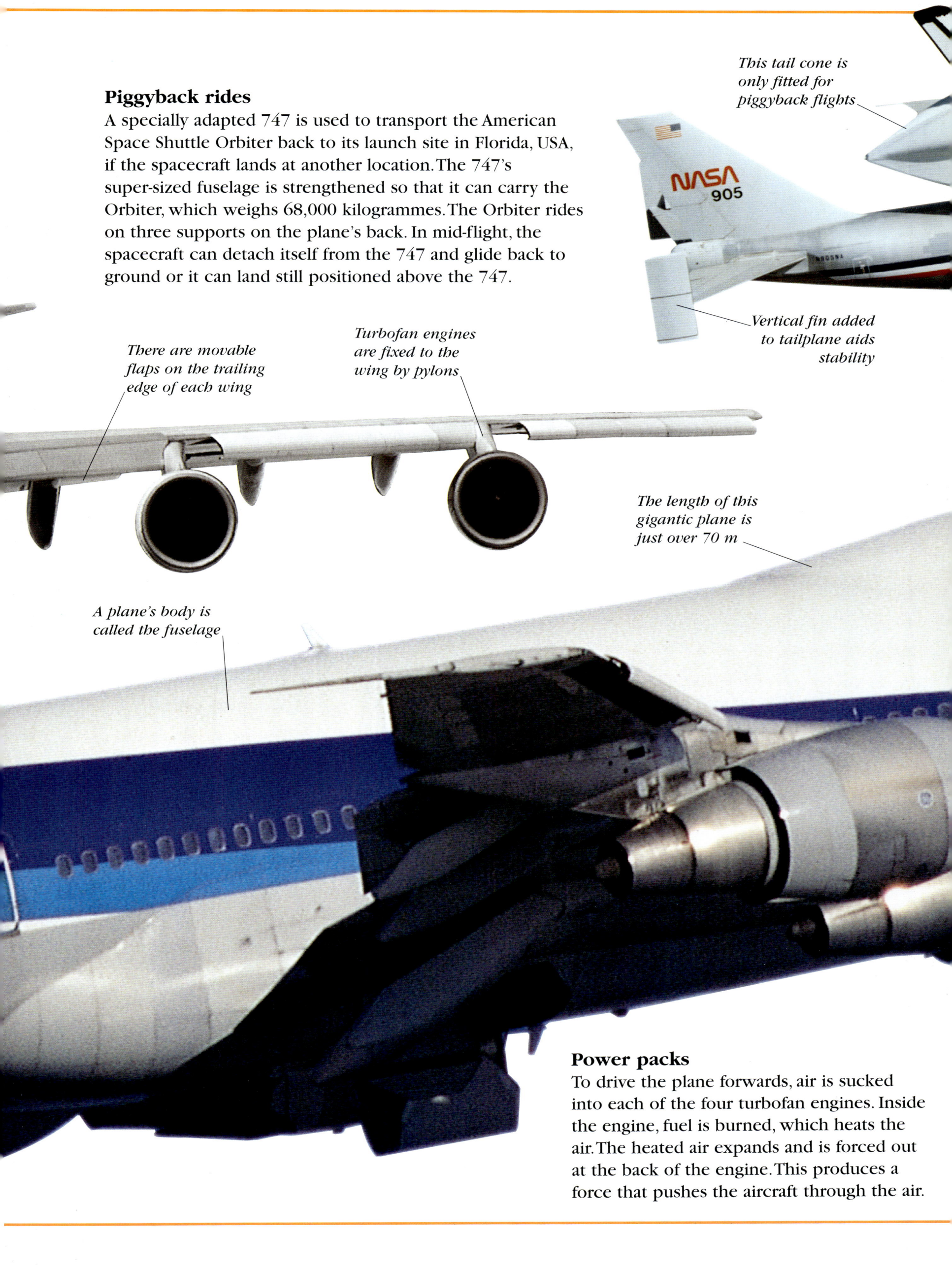

A specially adapted 747 is used to transport the American Space Shuttle Orbiter back to its launch site in Florida, USA, if the spacecraft lands at another location. The 747's super-sized fuselage is strengthened so that it can carry the Orbiter, which weighs 68,000 kilogrammes. The Orbiter rides on three supports on the plane's back. In mid-flight, the spacecraft can detach itself from the 747 and glide back to ground or it can land still positioned above the 747.

This tail cone is only fitted for piggyback flights

Vertical fin added to tailplane aids stability

There are movable flaps on the trailing edge of each wing

Turbofan engines are fixed to the wing by pylons

The length of this gigantic plane is just over 70 m

A plane's body is called the fuselage

Power packs

To drive the plane forwards, air is sucked into each of the four turbofan engines. Inside the engine, fuel is burned, which heats the air. The heated air expands and is forced out at the back of the engine. This produces a force that pushes the aircraft through the air.

Mobile crane

Mobile cranes are lifting machines on wheels, which means they can be driven to where they are needed. There are lots of different sizes – the larger the crane, the heavier the weight it can lift. The big picture shows a huge crane, which can lift four times its own weight.

Mobile cranes are often seen on building or road sites, lifting bulky loads.

Stretching out
Before this crane starts to lift heavy loads, an operator has to extend the legs, or outriggers. This helps to spread the weight of the crane and stops it from toppling over.

Outriggers stand 12 m apart

Outriggers rest on metal discs, called jacks

Outriggers tuck away when not in use

There are two engines – an engine here works the jib

An engine here drives the crane

Mast to strengthen jib when the jib is raised

Zoom action

This crane's arm, or jib, has three sections. These are extended to rise to 50 metres – or 140 metres if a special attachment is added. Once the jib is up, the hook block moves to pick up the load.

Jib

Pulley

Jib is extended from here

Warning lights flash when the crane moves

This hook block weighs more than a car

This is called the cathead

Lifting cable

Looping this cable around the cathead allows the crane to lift more

Larger hook blocks are used for heavier loads

This crane has 18 wheels

Three people can sit side by side in the cab

A metal rope, called a stay, holds the hook block to the cab for road travel

13

Icebreaker

When the water in a busy river or sea channel freezes over, a ship called an icebreaker goes to work. It's the only way to keep a channel open for other ships. Icebreakers have powerful engines that turn huge propellers, forcing the ship's strong hull through ice that may be over two metres thick.

An icebreaker rams through the thick ice before crushing the ice with its mighty weight.

Mighty ship
The width, or beam, of an icebreaker is much bigger than other sea-going ships. This enables an icebreaker to clear a passage through the ice that is wide enough for the ships to sail.

The captain controls the icebreaker from the bridge at the top of the ship

In dock, ropes pass through here, securing the ship to the harbour wall

A big icebreaker may be 30 m wide

The hull is made of thick steel

Ships have communication equipment that links to the shore via satellite

The front, or bow, drops straight down towards the ice

The back of a ship is called the stern

Crane for loading and unloading of supplies

Several metres of hull are beneath the waterline

A ship's propellers are beneath the water at the stern

Built to cut

Icebreakers have a special shape. The bow falls almost straight down to sea level, but runs sharply back just above the waterline. This acts like a huge knife to cut into the ice. The hull is made of steel that is several centimetres thick.

There may be more than 100 crew aboard a sea-going icebreaker, including engineers, radio operators, and cooks

Lifeboats hang at the sides to allow emergency evacuation if anything goes wrong

Giant dump truck

Giant dump trucks are used in quarries to move huge amounts of earth or rocks away from the quarry face. To do this they need powerful engines and enormous tipper bodies to haul the load. This giant dump truck has an engine that equals the strength of 1,400 horses!

This truck is almost half as long as a tennis court

A hefty metal plate protects the driver's cab from falling rocks or earth

The truck is four times the width of a car

Safety rail

Bits and pieces
Giant dump trucks are far too big to travel on ordinary roads when they move to a new site – even the tyres are taller than a horse. So the trucks have to be taken apart and loaded on to special transporters.

The driver has to climb a ladder to reach the cab

Bumper is about 1 m from the ground

Radiator grille

Air horn

Everything out!

When the truck is ready to dump its load, the body tips right up. Two massive arms, called hydraulic rams, push the tipper body up so that the load slides out. The driver operates the hydraulic rams from the safety of the cab. When this dump truck tips up, it reaches 11 metres. This dump truck can carry up to 150 tonnes of earth – that's as much as 30 elephants!

It takes just 15 seconds to raise the truck's body and dump its load.

Door to driver's cab

A green light shows when the truck is being loaded – a red light indicates when the truck is full

V-shaped tipper body is deeper than the height of a grown-up

Mud flap

Twin rear tyres on each side help support the load

17

Instant control
Water rains down on a fire through a nozzle at the end of the hose. Firefighters on the platform or on the ground control this flow. At its most powerful, the water can be pumped out at 4,550 litres per minute. That's the equivalent of almost 14,000 small cans of soft drink!

Spare water hoses

Equipment lockers contain items such as hammers, saws, and spades

This boom stretches up 25 m

Firefighters sit in this compartment on their way to a fire

Axes are often needed for getting into a building

Loose hoses are attached here

Fire engine

Fire engines are tough, hard-working machines. They are used for all kinds of jobs, from putting out fires to rescuing people trapped in high buildings. Some fire engines carry massive tanks of water, others have extendable ladders. The fire engine shown below is called a hydraulic platform, or snorkel. Its long arm, or boom, has a built-in water hose. Some booms can stretch to 62 metres.

A fire engine's boom can reach the top of a tall building to fight a fire.

Firefighters stand on this platform to fight a fire

One of four fold-up legs, which will extend to the ground before the boom is raised

Portable extension ladders provide instant access to a building

Warning light, which flashes when the fold-up leg is being placed into position

Fold-up leg

Locomotive

A locomotive has an engine that generates power to move a train of containers. Five or six big locomotives like these are powerful enough to make up trains hauling 80 or more containers hundreds of kilometres. The trains may stretch for two kilometres! Locomotives transport all kinds of goods, such as wheat, cars, metal, and coal.

Containers are attached to one another and hauled by a powerful locomotive.

Vital statistics
Locomotives are heavy machines, weighing an average of about 112 tonnes. Some weigh far more than this, at over 180 tonnes! This weight helps to keep the locomotive on the track.

Locomotives, such as this one, can travel at maximum speeds of about 120 kph

Most containers can carry about 86.7 tonnes

The engineer, or driver, sits in this cab

Locomotives have strong supporting frames – steel bars are used, which are 10 cm thick

Each train has an identifying number

Most locomotives are 15 m long – some are 24 m

Horse power
You would need 6,000 horses to replace a large, modern locomotive – just think how much food these horses would need! But an engine still needs feeding with fuel. Most locomotives gulp six litres every kilometre! The fuel tank, positioned underneath the frame, can contain up to 22,750 litres of fuel.

Concrete is sometimes added to the locomotive's frame to increase weight

To reach the cab, the crew has to climb this ladder

Powerful headlight

A protective steel plate, called a cowcatcher, pushes aside any debris on the line

Emergency light

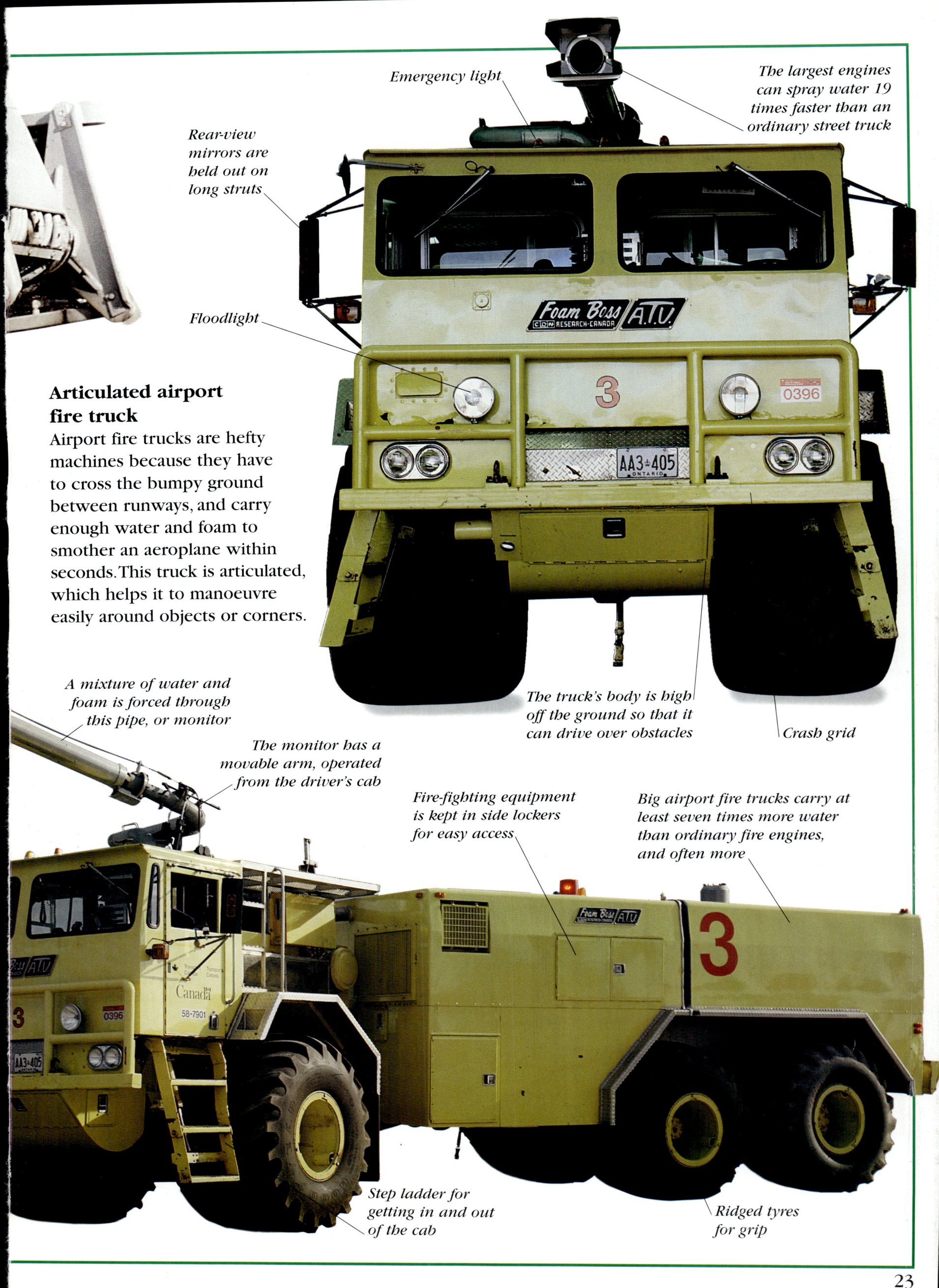

The largest engines can spray water 19 times faster than an ordinary street truck

Rear-view mirrors are held out on long struts

Floodlight

Articulated airport fire truck

Airport fire trucks are hefty machines because they have to cross the bumpy ground between runways, and carry enough water and foam to smother an aeroplane within seconds. This truck is articulated, which helps it to manoeuvre easily around objects or corners.

A mixture of water and foam is forced through this pipe, or monitor

The truck's body is high off the ground so that it can drive over obstacles

Crash grid

The monitor has a movable arm, operated from the driver's cab

Fire-fighting equipment is kept in side lockers for easy access

Big airport fire trucks carry at least seven times more water than ordinary fire engines, and often more

Step ladder for getting in and out of the cab

Ridged tyres for grip

23

Emergency lights and floodlights

A hose, 10 cm in diameter, runs the length of the boom

The boom takes just 78 seconds to fully unfold

Tinted glass reduces the sun's glare

Flashing warning light

Headlight

The tow eye is used to pull an obstacle, such as a car, out of the way

The siren is sounded when the engine is on an emergency call

An identifying number allows the fire chief to know the location of every fire engine

Cargo plane

This gigantic cargo plane has a name to match its odd shape – it is called a Beluga, after a white whale. When the cargo door is raised, its puffy body reveals a huge cave-like space, which can contain the wings or body of another plane. The cargo plane flies these parts from different places to a central factory to be put together.

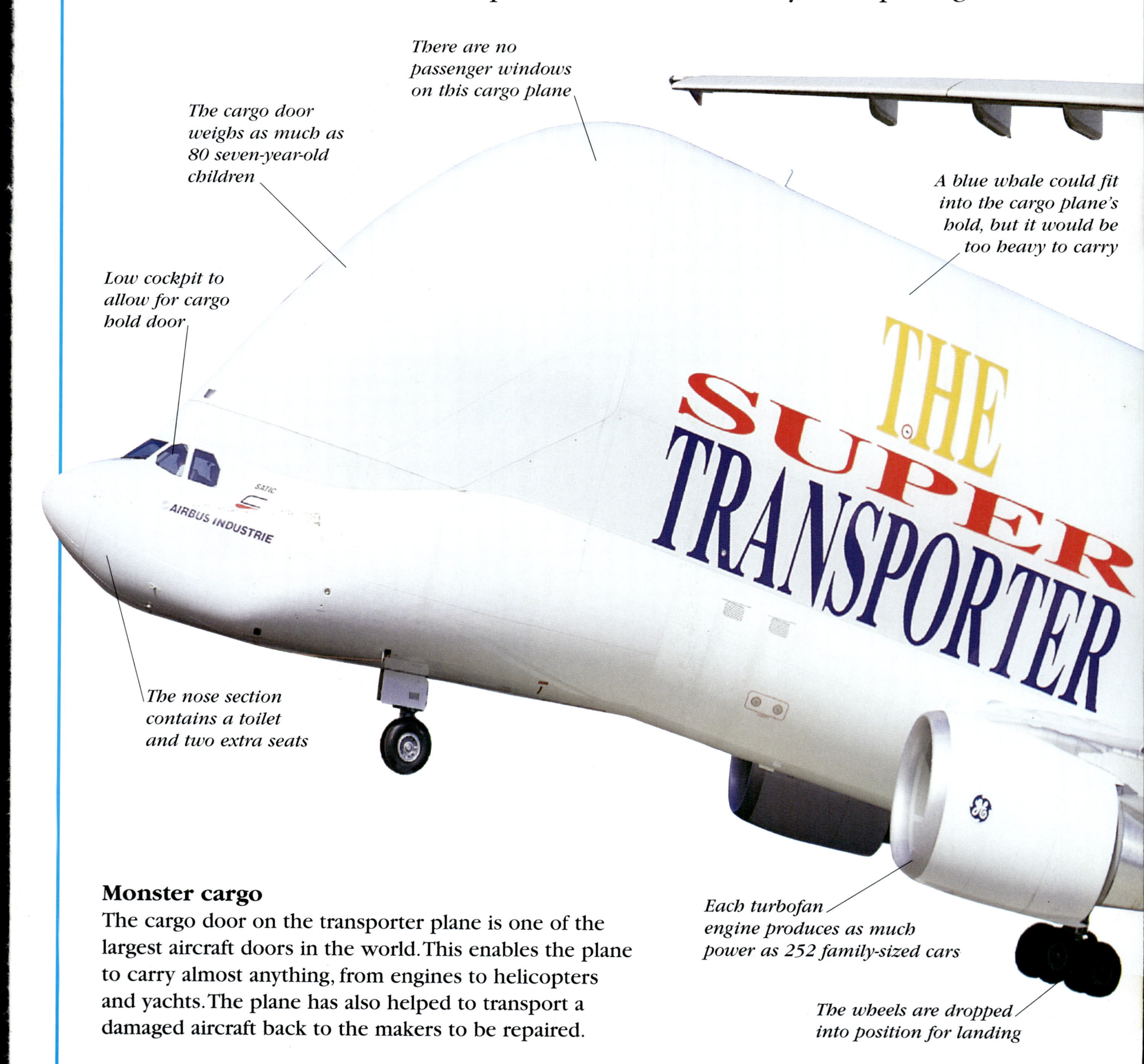

It takes just over an hour to load the transporter's monster cargo – here it is swallowing a helicopter!

The cargo door weighs as much as 80 seven-year-old children

There are no passenger windows on this cargo plane

A blue whale could fit into the cargo plane's hold, but it would be too heavy to carry

Low cockpit to allow for cargo hold door

The nose section contains a toilet and two extra seats

Each turbofan engine produces as much power as 252 family-sized cars

The wheels are dropped into position for landing

Monster cargo

The cargo door on the transporter plane is one of the largest aircraft doors in the world. This enables the plane to carry almost anything, from engines to helicopters and yachts. The plane has also helped to transport a damaged aircraft back to the makers to be repaired.

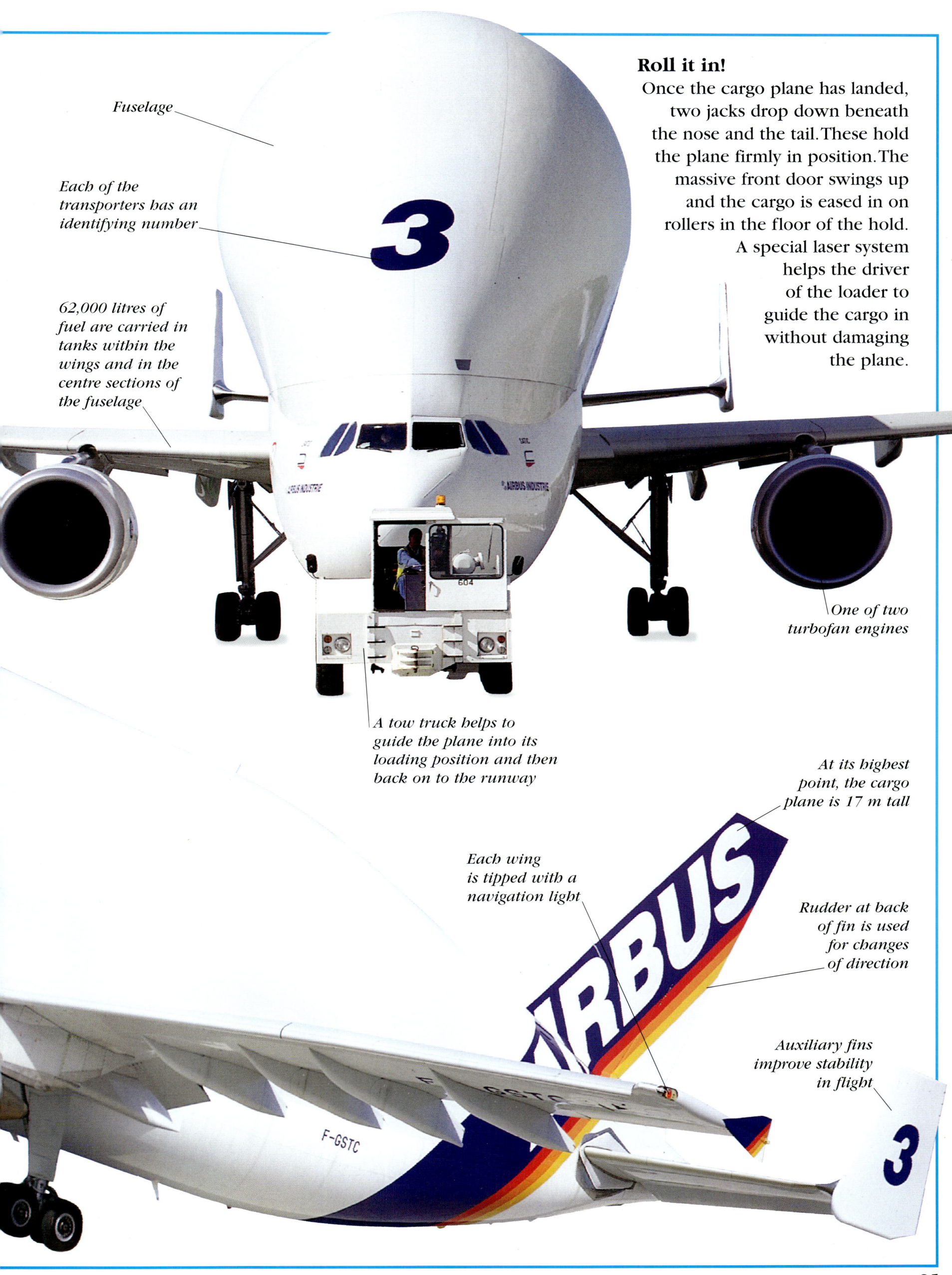

Fuselage

Each of the transporters has an identifying number

62,000 litres of fuel are carried in tanks within the wings and in the centre sections of the fuselage

Roll it in!
Once the cargo plane has landed, two jacks drop down beneath the nose and the tail. These hold the plane firmly in position. The massive front door swings up and the cargo is eased in on rollers in the floor of the hold. A special laser system helps the driver of the loader to guide the cargo in without damaging the plane.

One of two turbofan engines

A tow truck helps to guide the plane into its loading position and then back on to the runway

At its highest point, the cargo plane is 17 m tall

Each wing is tipped with a navigation light

Rudder at back of fin is used for changes of direction

Auxiliary fins improve stability in flight

Recovery truck

If a big truck has an accident, a heavy recovery truck has to tow it to a garage to be repaired. This recovery truck is equipped with a lifting system that can pull the equivalent of about 80 family-sized cars! To balance this weight, the truck's front bumper is made of solid steel.

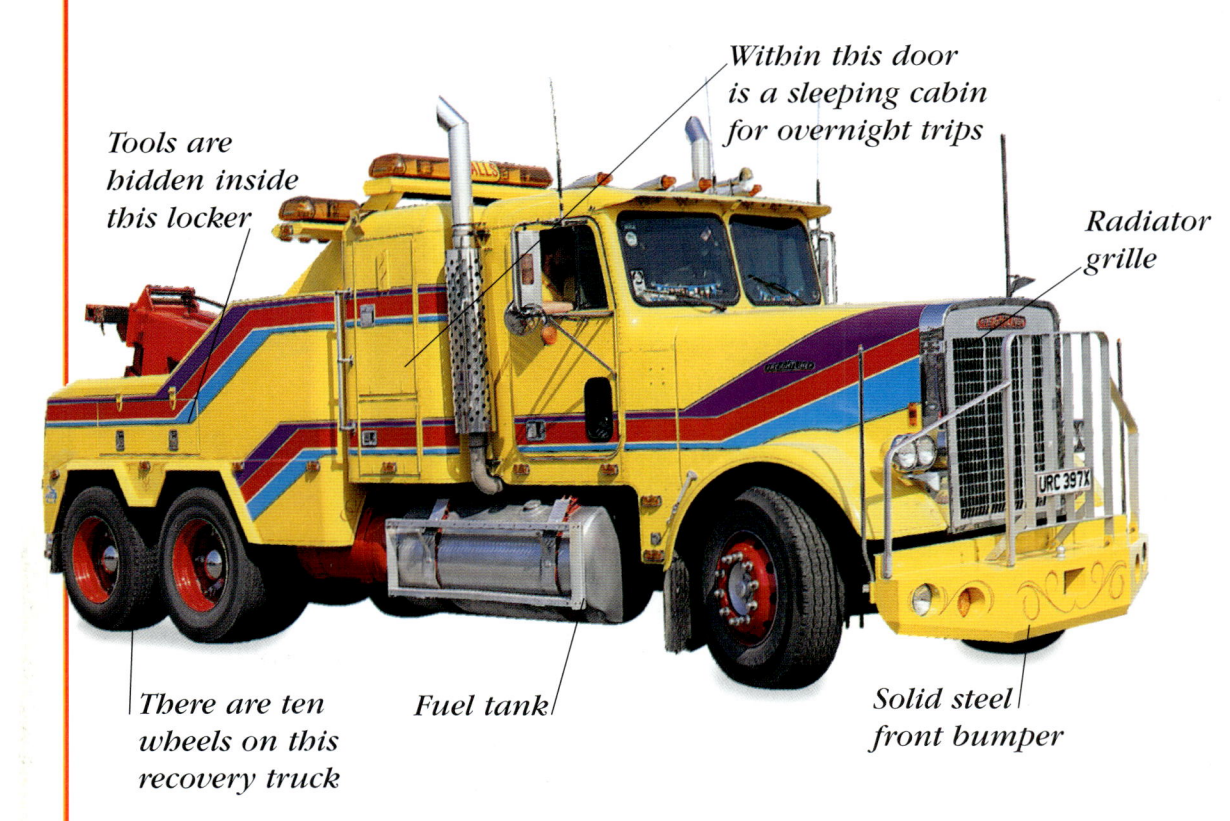

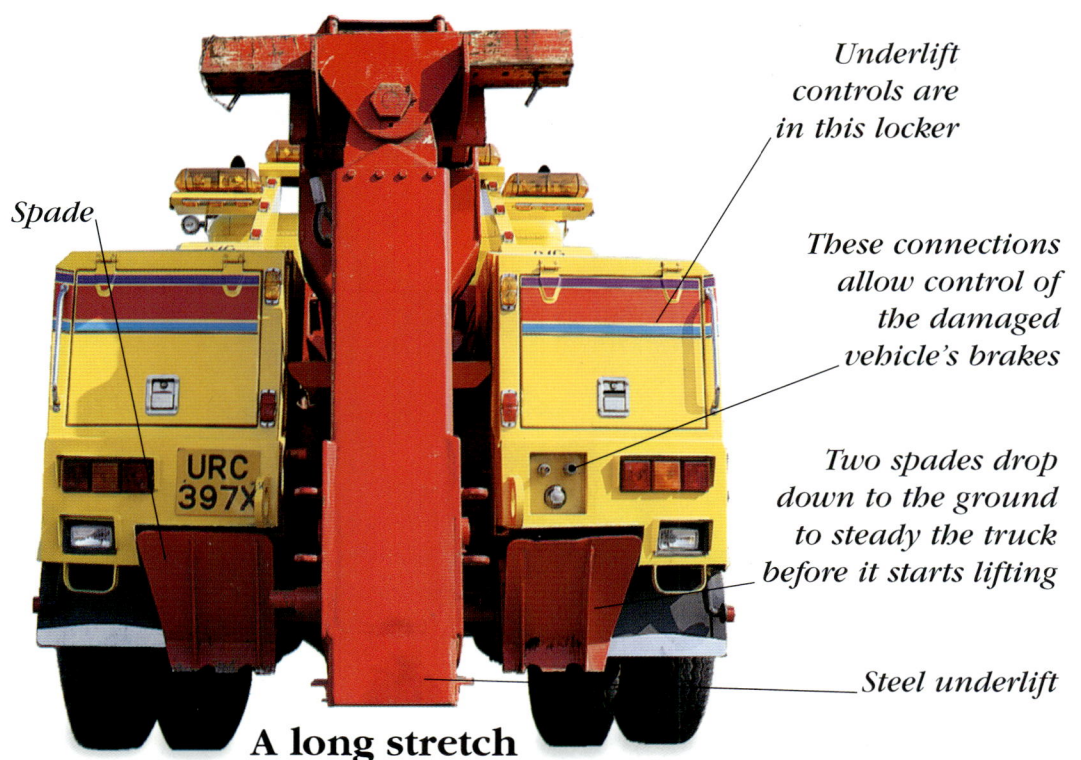

Tools are hidden inside this locker

Within this door is a sleeping cabin for overnight trips

Radiator grille

Rear-view mirror

The exhaust pipe has a protective cover

Side marker

Headlight

There are ten wheels on this recovery truck

Fuel tank

Solid steel front bumper

Spade

Underlift controls are in this locker

These connections allow control of the damaged vehicle's brakes

Two spades drop down to the ground to steady the truck before it starts lifting

Steel underlift

A long stretch
To rescue a vehicle, a recovery truck has to slide a long metal arm, called an underlift, beneath it. This stretches out about three metres to lift the damaged vehicle. The recovery truck flashes its hazard light as a warning to other road users to keep clear while it is working.

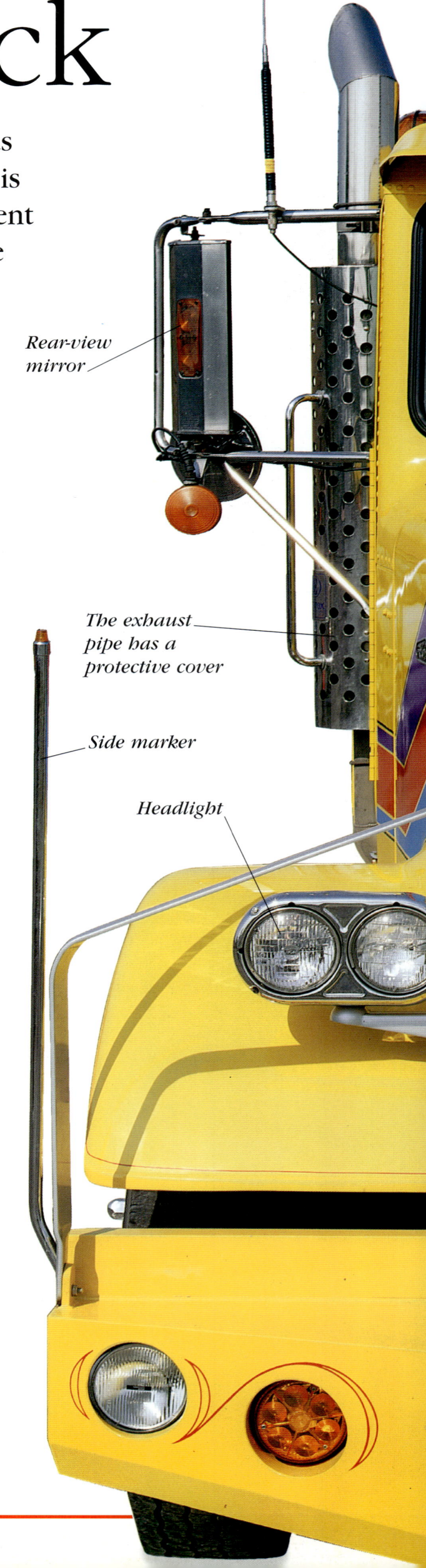

Hazard light

Radio aerial

Width test
Two side markers show the width of the truck in narrow spaces. They are even tipped with lights.

Tractor

This tractor is hauling a trailer next to a combine harvester. The corn is cut and blown into the trailer.

If you visit a farm, you will usually see a tractor. These tough machines are a farmer's best friend – they help with all kinds of jobs. Some large tractors can equal the strength of more than 350 horses, though few tractors need to be this powerful.

A tractor cab seats one person

Powerful headlights allow the tractor to work at night

The engine is underneath the bonnet

Machinery can be attached at the front

Counterweight

A balancing act
Tractors pull heavy trailers so weights have to be added to counterbalance these trailers. The metal counterweight attached to the front of this tractor weighs about as much as eight children.

This tractor is towing a plough

The plough will be dragged up and down the field to turn over the earth

The grooves are deeper than the length of your finger

28

Waste gases pass through the exhaust pipe

There is only one central windscreen wiper

Rear-view mirror

Which job today?
Tractors can be linked up at the front or the back with various machines or trailers. This enables a farmer to carry out different tasks around the farm, from lifting wooden pallets to ploughing a field. The driver can hook up to a trailer without leaving the cab.

The cab's temperature can be controlled by the driver

The cab has large windscreens, giving the driver good all-round vision

The tractor's body sits high off the ground to stop it from being damaged by large rocks

Steps make it easy to reach the cab

Grooved tyres prevent the tractor from getting stuck in a muddy field

Water may be put in the tyres to help them grip on slippery surfaces

The front wheels help the driver to steer the tractor

29

Articulated truck

Big articulated trucks are a common sight as they transport goods around a country, picking up and making deliveries to shops, seaports, and airports. These powerful trucks are designed so that they can haul different types of trailers, big or small. This is the front of an articulated truck.

Single bunk compartment for long trips

Grab rail helps the driver climb up into the cab

The front section is called the tractor unit

Linking up
The tractor unit is built to join up with different trailers. This enables the driver to deliver one trailer and pick up another. Some tractor units can haul three or four trailers at once, making long "road trains".

Trailer will link up to tractor unit above these wheels

Treads on each tyre help grip the road

Steps to cab have a non-slip surface

Heat shields guard the exhaust pipes

The curved collar cuts wind resistance

There are two exhaust pipes

A visor helps to protect the driver from the sun's glare

Articulated trucks can haul trailers that can carry anything from food to animals. This truck unit is hauling a heavily loaded open trailer.

Time saver
Truck drivers have to make long journeys and don't want to keep stopping to refuel, so a truck has a huge fuel tank. Some carry enough fuel to fill a car's tank 40 times!

The truck's aerodynamic shape helps the truck to move smoothly as it speeds along

There are ten wheels on the tractor unit

Bumper helps protect the truck

Glossary

Aerial
A device for transmitting or receiving radio signals.

Aerodynamic shape
A vehicle may have a sleek shape to help it move through the air. This enables the vehicle to go much faster.

Air conditioning
A means of cooling down an area, such as a vehicle's cab.

Air horn
A horn through which air is squeezed to make a loud warning noise.

Articulated truck
A truck that has two sections: the front containing the engine and cab, and a trailer containing goods.

Bonnet
The metal covering that goes over a vehicle's engine.

Boom
The back section of a hydraulic arm, which works the front section.

Bow
The front of a ship.

Bumper
A protective bar attached to the front and back of a vehicle.

Cab
The part of a truck or locomotive that contains the driver's seat and all the machine's controls.

Cargo
Goods that are transported from one place to another.

Cockpit
The small cabin at the front of an aircraft or racing car that houses the controls.

Counterweight
A balance to a heavy weight.

Cowcatcher
A metal grid in front of a locomotive engine that clears obstacles on a railway line.

Engine
An engine burns fuel to make a vehicle work.

Exhaust pipe
A metal pipe through which waste gases leave the engine.

Fuel
The solid, liquid, or gas material that powers an engine.

Fuselage
A plane's body.

Hull
The lower shell of a ship or boat.

Hydraulic ram
Liquid is pumped through a metal tube to move it forwards or backwards. This moves the parts that may be attached to the tube.

Jacks
Metal feet used to steady a machine.

Jib
A crane's extending metal arm.

Outriggers
A vehicle's legs, which extend and rest on the ground to steady it.

Propeller
A bladed shaft, which revolves to propel a ship or aircraft forwards.

Radar
A navigation system that sends out radio waves to locate a position.

Radiator
Hot water from the engine is pumped through a vehicle's radiator to cool the engine down.

Rear-view mirror
A mirror on the side of a vehicle that shows a driver what is behind.

Rudder
Movement of the rudder makes a plane, ship, or boat turn left or right.

Satellite
A machine in orbit that transmits signals to and receives them from Earth.

Shock absorbers
These lessen the impact of bumps in the road to give the occupants of a vehicle a smoother ride.

Stern
The back of a ship.

Turbofan engine
A jet engine that contains a fan, adding to the engine's thrust.

Tyre
The rubber ring that is fitted around a wheel.

Undercarriage
The mechanism that holds a plane's wheels.